Cars & Stars

Daryl West

SunRise

SunRise

First published in Great Britain in 2022 by SunRise

SunRise Publishing Ltd
Kemp House
152–160 City Road
London EC1V 2NX

ISBN 978-1-9144890-4-4

A CIP catalogue record for this book is available from the British Library.

Typeset in Minion Pro.

Contents

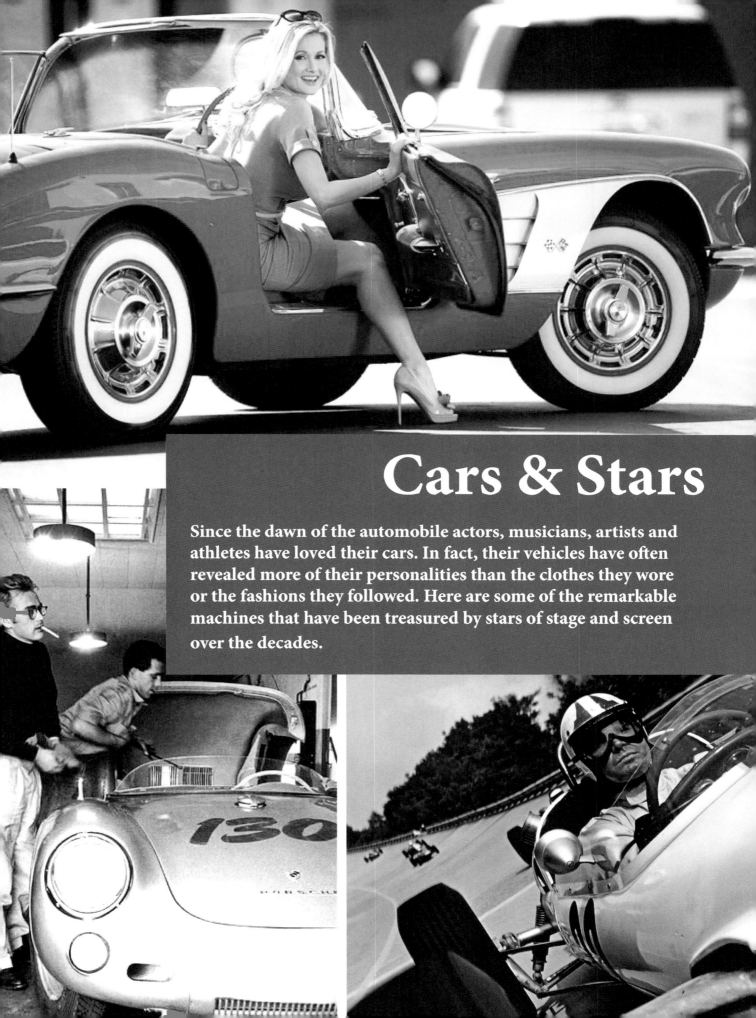

Cars & Stars

Since the dawn of the automobile actors, musicians, artists and athletes have loved their cars. In fact, their vehicles have often revealed more of their personalities than the clothes they wore or the fashions they followed. Here are some of the remarkable machines that have been treasured by stars of stage and screen over the decades.

stars who raced

In 1969 Paul Newman starred in *Butch Cassidy and the Sundance Kid*. The movie marked the high point of his acting career but, at the very peak of his success, he surprised critics by saying: 'Behind the wheel of a car, is the only place I've ever felt graceful.'

Newman was neither the first nor the last actor to love cars more than he loved movies. He took up motor racing at forty-six and raced for the last time, shortly before his death from cancer, at the age of eighty-three. His love of racing may have been sparked by the 1969 film *Winning,* in which he played a racing driver. To prepare for the film, he trained at a high-performance driving school, and went on to compete in sports car races for the rest of his life. He formed the successful Newman/Haas Racing team with his friend Carl Haas, winning more than 100 races and eight Driver's Championships in the IndyCar Series.

'Behind the wheel of
a car, is the only place
I've ever felt graceful.'

Paul Newman

9

Left: Paul Newman's love for motor sport may have been inspired by the 1969 movie, Winning.

Right: Paul Newman is shown a new Ferrari at the company's Modena headquarters by CEO Jean Todt, in 2006.

Below: Paul Newman's wife, Joanne Woodward, with her Austin-Healey 3000.

Steve McQueen

I n the 1968 movie, *Bullitt,* Steve McQueen drove a green Ford Mustang GT390 which would become, arguably, the most iconic car ever to appear on screen. Two were specially built for the film: one was scrapped and the other preserved. McQueen tried hard to buy it but the custodian turned him down. The car did not finally come under the hammer until 2020, when it fetched a staggering $3.4M, the record price for any Mustang. McQueen, however, went on to acquire one of the most impressive automobile collections to be owned by any actor.

His Jaguar XKSS, which he nicknamed *The Green Rat* was one of only sixteen examples to survive a fire at Jaguar's factory. Today, Steve's beautiful car can be found in the Petersen Automotive Museum.

cars & stars

One of McQueen's favourite racing cars was a lightwieght Lotus 11 which he raced many times and won a few trophies in, among them first place in a 1959 race at Santa Barbara. He later bought a Porsche 908 Spyder in which he finished second in the 1970 Sebring 12-hour race. His insurance company refused to let him drive in the 1971 film, *Le Mans*, but his Porsche served as a camera car.

Above: Steve McQueen and film director John Sturgess admire McQueen's Jaguar XKSS during filming of Le Mans.
Below: McQueen bought this Ferrari 250G Lusso for his first wife, Neile Adams.

James Dean

More than sixty years after James Dean's death, his legend endures. He only made three films, but all are considered classics and Hollywood is still searching for the 'new' James Dean. He was just twenty-four in September 1955 when his Porsche 550 Spyder collided with a station wagon, claiming the young star's life.

His first sports car had been a second-hand 1953 MG TD and he later bought a 1955 Triumph TR5 Trophy and a new 1955 Porsche 550 Speedster. He raced the Porsche at Palm Springs, finishing first in a novice race and second overall in the main event. At Bakersfield, he finished first in class and third overall. From June to mid-September of 1955, he was filming *Giant* and Warner Brothers barred him from racing until shooting was over. As soon as he was free to race again, he bought a new Porsche 550 Spyder which he named *Little Bastard* and entered it for the Salinas Road Race scheduled for 1–2 October. The fatal crash occurred on his way to that race, just nine days after he took delivery of the car.

James Garner

When James Garner was practising for his role in the 1966 movie, *Grand Prix*, Graham Hill told him he had the makings of a real racing driver, and Garner later competed in races himself. Of the 32 professional racing drivers who participated or were seen in the film, *Grand Prix*, five died in racing accidents within two years and another five in the following ten years.

Steve McQueen was the early choice for the lead role, but he fell out with the producer. McQueen did not speak to his replacement (friend, and next-door neighbour, James Garner) for the next four years, but he later starred in another racing movie, *Le Mans* (1971).

rock stars & their cars

In 1960s London, the humble Austin 7 Mini was the height of chic for Paul McCartney and Cathy McGowan. Paul's then girlfriend, Jane Asher, was happy with a 1950s Ford Anglia, but George Harrison preferred an Aston Martin DB5.

Janis Joplin chose psychedelic paintwork for her 1964 Porsche 356, as did John Lennon for his 1965 Rolls-Royce Phantom V. Rod Stewart was cool with a Lamborghini Miura, and Mick Jagger with a Morgan Plus 8, but when Keith Moon lent his Ferrari 246 Dino to a friend, he got it back as a total wreck!

Bruce Springsteen with his 1960 Chevrolet Corvette C1 Convertible
and Mick Jagger with a 1966 Aston Martin DB5.

Elvis Presley and Ann-Margret in an Elva-Maserati Mark VI.
Grace Jones in a Ferrari 488.

Pink Floyd founder Nick Mason's Ferrari 250 GTO is said to be the world's most valuable car. Bought for £35,000 in the 1970s, it is now thought to be worth around £50 million.

the name is Bond ...

In Ian Fleming's novels, James Bond famously drove a 1931 4.5 Litre Blower Bentley, 'Bond drove it hard and well and with an almost sensual pleasure.'

The 1964 movie, *Goldfinger*, however, would imortalise Sean Connery's Aston Martin DB5. The legendary car went on to appear in *Thunderball* (1965), *GoldenEye* (1995), *Tomorrow Never Dies* (1997), *Casino Royale* (2006), *Skyfall* (2012), *Spectre* (2015) and *No Time To Die* (2021).

Roger Moore drove an amphibious Lotus Esprit S1 with Barbara Bach in *The Spy Who Loved Me* (1977), armed with surface-to-air missiles, a cement jet sprayer, mines and torpedoes.

stars of the silent screen

From the earliest days of Hollywood, movie stars chose their cars with as much care as their homes or clothes. Rudolph Valentino (with dog) favoured a Voisin C5, Douglas Fairbanks and Mary Pickford settled for a more modest Ford Model A, and Buster Keaton got a ticket in his Austin 10. Greta Garbo, however, went upscale with an enormous Rolls-Royce Phantom 1.

29

Austin-Healey

der.englaender

When the designer and rally driver Donald Healey joined forces with the Austin division of the British Motor Corporation, the result was some of the most stylish and succesful sports cars of the mid-twentieth century.

(Clockwise) Ann-Margret, and Anthony Franciosa in *The Pleasure Seekers* (1964). Lewis Hamilton at the Canadian Grand Prix. Clint Eastwood with his Austin-Healey 100M. George Harrison and Paul McCartney in a Sprite and Harrison Ford with his 1966 Austin-Healey 3000 Mk III.

When racing driver Carroll Shelby shoehorned an American V8 into AC's beautiful Cobra chassis, a legend was born.

(Clockwise) Carroll Shelby's signature. Lewis Hamilton's 1966 Shelby Cobra 427. Taylor Swift attacks a Cobra in a music video and Steve McQueen takes delivery of a new Cobra from Carroll Shelby himself.

Shelby Cobra

E-Type Jaguar

The Jaguar E-Type (XKE in the US) is arguably the most iconic sports car ever built. Launched in 1961, it took the world by storm, has never gone out of fashion and even Enzo Ferrari admitted it was beautiful.

(Clockwise) Elton John, George Best, Peter O'Toole, Audrey Hepburn, Catherine Zeta-Jones, Fictional FBI agent Jerry Cotton and Anita Eckberg.

At the 1948 London Motor Show Jaguar launched the XK120 sports car using the new XK engine designed by Jaguar Chief Engineer William Heynes. Followed by the XK140 and XK150, they quickly became saught after classics and today get record prices at auction.

(Clockwise) Miles Davis, Clint Eastwood, Roger Moore, Van Johnson, Robbie Coltrane, Mamie Van Doren and Richard Hammond.

Jaguar XK120/40/50

Cadillac

From the company's beginnings in 1902, Cadillac forged a reputation for luxury and technical excellence. By the time General Motors took over the business in 1909, they were already America's most prestigious autombile brand.

(Clockwise) Elvis Presley with a 1958 Cadillac Eldorado. Dollie Parton with her 1964 Cadillac Coupe DeVille.

Diana Dors and Sugar Ray Robinson with 1955 Cadillac convertibles.

(Clockwise) Angie Dickinson in a 1962 Cadillac. Robert Wagner Jr polishes a 1947 model. Muhammad Ali and his mother Odessa O'Grady Clay in a 1963 Eldorado. Joan Crawford in a 1932 Cadillac Fleetwood and Marilyn Monroe in a 1954 convertible.

Rolls-Royce

When engineer Henry Royce merged his electrical and mechanical business with the London car dealer Charles Rolls, they created the world's most prestigious brand. Rolls-Royce would become a global synonym for quality not only in cars but in practically everything. For more than a century both the double R logo and the Spirit of Ecstasy bonnet emblem have been instantly recognised across the world.

Both Michael Caine and Cardi B acquired their first Rolls-Royces before they had learned to drive. Sir Michael was fifty before he finally passed his test.

Sammy Davis Jr in London in 1963, and Beyoncé in New York in a 1959 Rolls-Royce Silver Cloud II convertible.

The first Mercedes-Benz 300 SL was a Grand Prix racing car built in 1952 with no intention of developing a street version. In 1954, an American importer, Max Hoffman, suggested a street version of the 300 SL for customers in the United States where the market for the luxury cars was booming. The 1954 'Gull Wing' 300 SL was an instant success, and the SL has been through many variations and improvements until the present day.

Actor Patrick Duffy (aka Bobby Ewing) with a 450 SL and Formula One driver Nico Rosberg with his beloved 300 SL.

Mercedes-Benz SL

Princess Diana in her 500 SL, and Sophia Loren in the 300 SL that her husband, Carlo Ponti, gave her as a birthday present.

(Clockwise) Katy Perry and Orlando Bloom. German football star Gerd Müller. Sophia Loren gets out to push! Dutch super-model Lara Stone in a Calvin Klein campaign.

Porsche

SIERRA LEONE Le 14500

Porsche 550 Spyder   2020

65TH MEMORIAL ANNIVERSARY OF
JAMES DEAN

Doctor Ferdinand Porsche had not previously designed an automobile when Germany's pre-war government commissioned him to produce a 'People's Car'. The resulting Volkswagen Beetle became the most successful and popular family car of all time. He was imprisoned after the war but his son, Ferry, continued to make cars under the Porsche name. The Porsche 911, which was first built in 1963, has gone through eight metamorphoses but has remained one of the most iconic sports cars of all time.

(Clockwise) Patrick Dempsey with his 1963 356. James Dean's 550 Spyder. Jeremy Clarkson with a 918 Spyder. Michael Fassbender with a racing 911. Emma Radacanu with a 911 GT3. The 2022 movie *Top Gun: Maverick* features a 1973 911 S, pictured with Jennifer Connelly and Tom Cruise.

Ferrari

(Clockwise) Gordon Ramsay, Ralph Lauren and Chris Evans all have collections of Ferraris. Kylie Jenner poses in a LaFerrari-Aperta 488 Spider, and Lewis Hamilton parks his LaFerrari.

Enzo Ferrari made his reputation as a racing driver for Alfa Romeo, winning his first Grand Prix in 1923. The Scuderia Ferrari racing team he created originally raced Alfa Romeo cars with great success. In 1947 he began to build racing cars under his own name and later built street cars in order to finance his Formula One Team. Today, Ferrari is considered to be the world's most powerful automotive brand. So exclusive is the name that the company actually vets potential owners and turns down those they feel don't deserve one of their cars!

Aston Martin

The Aston Martin company was founded in 1913 by Lionel Martin and Robert Bamford. But it was David Brown, who took over in 1947, who built their reputation as constructors of fast, luxury grand touring cars. James Bond's use of a DB5 in several movies from 1964 onwards, along with royal warrants, helped to cement their reputation and today they remain one of the most prestigious automobile brands in the world.

(Clockwise) Daniel Craig favours a DB10. Prince William chose dad's DB6 for his wedding to Kate. David Beckham prized his AMV8 Volante. Prince Charles has owned his DB6 Volante since 1970 and Tom Brady has an Aston Martin Vanquish S Volante.

Ford Thunderbird

Ford unveiled the first Thunderbird in 1954. Like General Motors, who had previously launched their Corvette, Ford hoped to tap into the growing popularity of European sports cars in America. The car was immediately popular and hugely outsold the Corvette. Although the Thunderbird was discontinued in 1957, Ford had already sold more than 50,000 examples and the car remains an icon to this day. Natalie Wood, Marilyn Monroe, Arthur Miller, Debbie Reynolds, Clark Gable and Frank Sinatra all became proud owners.

Chevrolet Corvette

The Chevrolet Corvette, first launched in 1953, has gone through eight versions, remains the only two-seat sports car built by a major US car manufacturer, and is still Chevrolet's halo vehicle. At one time NASA astronauts were given new Corvettes which were replaced each year.

Holy Madison, Alan Shepard (far right) Steve McQueen, Kendall Jenner and Mario Andretti all love their 'Vettes'.

Brigitte Bardot

In the late 1950s and early 1960s Brigitte Bardot (or BB as she became known) was France's best-known sex symbol, and a poster girl for the French film industry. Often photographed in St Tropez, her favourite car was an unpretentious Renault Floride Cabriolet, but she later bought a 1967 Lancia.

Raquel Welch

In 1966, Raquel Welch appeared in the movie *One Million Years BC*. Although she only had three lines of dialogue, she instantly became an international sex symbol. Often photographed with cars, her personal transport was a 1965 Ferrari 275 GTS. Early in her career she helped publicise American motor sport.

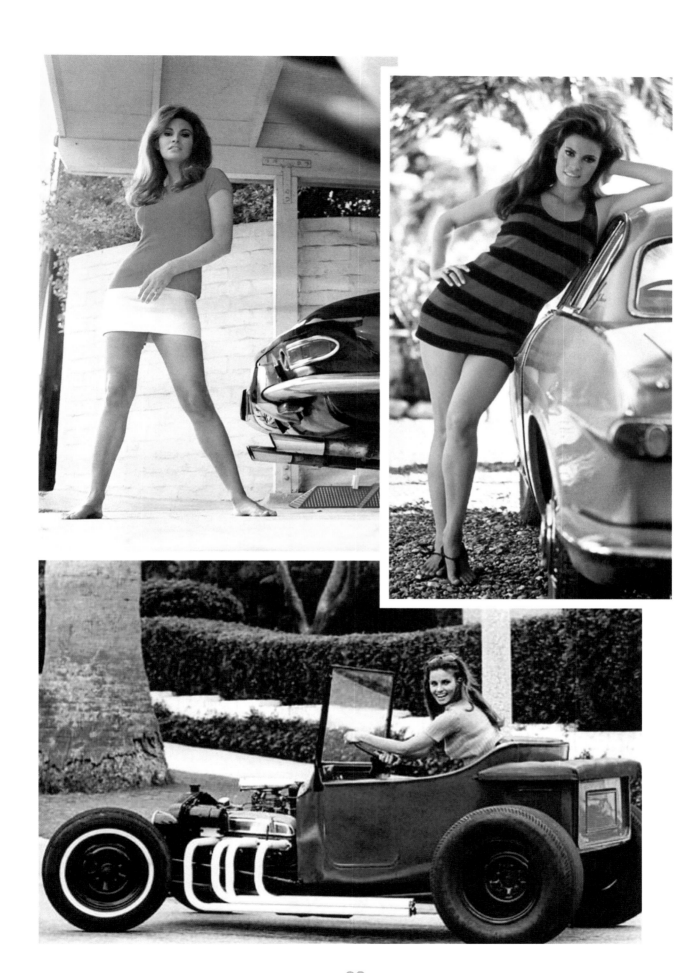

Stars with modest cars ...

When photographed by *Life*, Jack Nicholson drove a convertible Volkswagen Beetle. Tom Hanks prefers a down-to-earth Toyota Land Cruiser and Mark Zuckerberg's transport is a modest Acura TSX. Meryl Streep and Helena Bonham Carter went for Fiat 500s and Jennifer Lawrence drives a Volkswagen Eos.

Stars with tasteful cars ...

Some stars choose cars whose personalities fit them like a glove: (Clockwise) Cary Grant in a 1961 Citroën DS 19 Décapotable. Jean Harlow in a 1932 Packard Candid. Paris Hilton in her Mercedes McLaren SLR. Humphrey Bogart and Audrey Hepburn in a Nash-Healey Roadster and Humphrey Bogart, Stephen Bogart and Lauren Bacall in their Jaguar XK120.

Index

Printed in Poland
by Amazon Fulfillment
Poland Sp. z o.o., Wrocław
26 July 2022

11093e24-f499-457d-92b7-bb5fa26950d6R01